# R. Gupta's®

# MY FIRST

# Essays & Letters Book

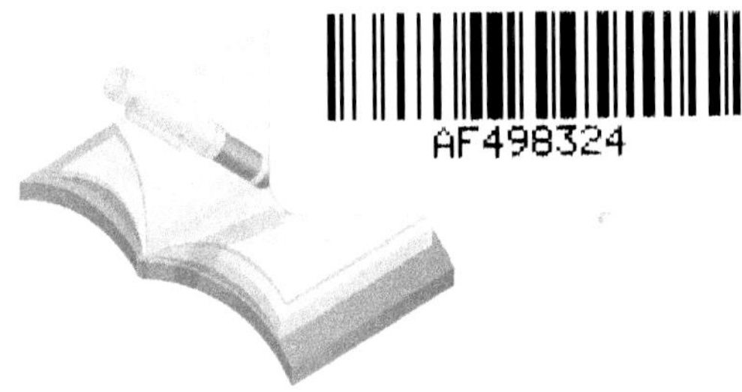

*RPH Editorial Board*

**Ramesh Publishing House, New Delhi**

**Published by**

O.P. Gupta *for* Ramesh Publishing House

**Admin. Office**

12-H, New Daryaganj Road, Opp. Officers' Mess,
New Delhi-110002 ✆ 23261567, 23275224, 23275124

E-mail: info@rameshpublishinghouse.com
Website: www.rameshpublishinghouse.com

**Showroom**

● Balaji Market, Nai Sarak, Delhi-6 ✆ 23253720, 23282525
● 4457, Nai Sarak, Delhi-6, ✆ 23918938



17th Edition: 1708

Book Code: R-1041

ISBN: 978-81-7812-632-6

HSN Code: 49011010

# Contents

# APPLICATIONS



# LETTERS

## MYSELF (A GIRL)

I am Garima. My surname is Swami. My father has given me this name. I am eight years old. I am a student of class three. My father is an engineer and my mother is an interior designer.

My father helps and guides me in my studies. My mother cooks tasty food for me. I like watching cartoons on television. I like drawing cartoon sketches. I do exercise every morning. I also like playing games on the computer. I am good at studies. My parents love me a lot and I also love them very much.

❑ ❑ ❑

# MYSELF (A BOY)

My name is Sarvagya. I am a boy. I am ten years old.

I study in Springdales School, Pusa Road. I am a student of class IVth. My school is near to my house as I live in Patel Nagar. I respect and obey my teachers.

My father is a doctor and my mother is a school teacher. I love and respect my parents. They also love me very much. I like cycling and playing cricket. I also like watching cartoons on T.V. I would like to become a cricketer when I grow up.

# MY SCHOOL

I study in Army Public School at Dhaula Kuan. It is a big school. The building of my school is very huge. It has fifty

classrooms. There is a reception, library, staff rooms and Principal's office. There are clean toilets for boys and girls on every floor separately.

A big assembly hall is also there. It has a big play ground. There is also a separate kids room and a medical room.

About 1500 students study in my school. The teachers of our school are highly educated and hard working. It is one of the best schools of our city.

# OUR SCHOOL LIBRARY

Our school has a big library. It has many big almirahs for books. It also has many long tables and chairs. There are thousands of books on various subjects. The Library also contains daily newspapers, magazines and periodicals. We borrow books from our school library. Library Card is distributed among students.

The librarian takes care of the library and also guides us to choose the right book. All the books are arranged very systematically. The teachers and the students come to the library to read the books. We all are expected to abide by the rules of the library. ❑ ❑ ❑

# MY FIRST DAY AT SCHOOL

I was a bit nervous on my first day at school. I still remember that I was five years old then. My father took me to the school. There was a friendly interaction between me and my class teacher. And I was admitted to class 1$^{st}$.

My class teacher was polite and energetic. She asked my name and welcomed me in a very sweet voice. I was offered a seat in the first row. There were many coloured toys in the classroom. In the games period I played with the other students of my class. When the school was over my father came to take me home. It was a very joyful day.

# MY CLASSROOM

I am a student of class IVth. There are thirty students in my class. My classroom is very big and spacious. It has two doors and six windows.

There are four fans in my classroom. It is well lighted. The black-board is big and well painted. The walls are white and clean. Maps, charts and pictures are well decorated on the display boards.

The desks we sit on are comfortable. There is a desk and a chair for the teacher also. There is also an almirah in my classroom. We all keep it neat and clean.

# MY FAVOURITE TEACHER

There are many teachers in my school. They teach different subjects to different classes. I like all my teachers but Mrs. Anjali Sen is my favourite teacher. She teaches

us English. I like her because of her good qualities and gentle nature. She is very helpful. She is always ready to solve our problems.

She is very hardworking and sweet by nature. She has a deep knowledge of her subject. All of us enjoy attending her class. She is respected by all the students of our school. ❑ ❑ ❑

    M.F. Essays-2

# SPORTS DAY IN OUR SCHOOL

Our school organizes the annual sports day in the month of February every year. It is a big event. There is a big crowd of  students and parents. We always have a famous person as our Chief Guest.

A variety of sports like racing, high jump, long jump, javelin throw, disc throw, obstacle racing, tug of war, judo etc are held on this day. The winners are cheered and applauded. In the end all the winners are awarded prizes by the Chief Guest.

# THE ANNUAL FUNCTION

Annual function is one of the most important events of our school. It is held in the month of March every year. Last year the Deputy Commissioner of Police of our area presided over the function.

The function was held in our school's auditorium. Carpets were spread, benches and chairs were arranged to sit on. Many programmes were performed. The Principal read out the annual report. The chief guest distributed the prizes. Then he made a short speech. The Principal thanked all the persons present there and the function ended.

❏ ❏ ❏

# THE GAME I LIKE MOST

Playing games is important for us. It keeps mind and body healthy. There are two types of games—indoor and outdoor. Indoor games are badminton, chess,  table-tennis etc. and outdoor games are cricket, football, hockey etc.

But the game I like the most is cricket. It is also known as the gentlemen's game. There are two teams, each having eleven players. One team bats while the other takes up fielding. There are three forms of cricket—test, one-day and twenty-twenty. It is technical as well as a mind game. The twist and turns of this game is its speciality. It is the most popular game in India.

# THE RECESS PERIOD

In the school, recess is a welcome break for all of us. We all start feeling a bit tired and hungry by  that time. It re-energies us. My recess period begins after the fourth period.

Every student waits eagerly for it. In the recess, students eat their lunch and play with their classmates. Many students can be seen gathering at canteen. Groups of students at various corners can be seen. When the recess period is over we all come back in the classroom and study starts again.

# A SCHOOL PICNIC

To go to a picnic from school is really a joy. Last Friday, all three sections of my class were taken to Nehru Planetarium at the Teen Murti. We assembled in our school in the morning.

There were many buses waiting  for us. We had fruits and other eatables with us in our picnic bags. Very soon we all left for the picnic.

We saw many stars, planets etc. over there. Teachers gave us various information about the Planet and Stars. Our knowledge was enhanced. By the evening we returned to the school. It was an unforgettable experience for all of us.

# MY SCHOOL PEON

Pyarelal is our school peon. He is tall and slim. He is not much educated still he is wise. He always wears his grey uniform.

Pyarelal is always smiling and cheerful. He is obedient. He can always be seen sitting on the stool outside the Principal's office. He keeps the Principal's office neat and clean. He is ready to help anytime. He carries out the orders of the Principal. He is busy all the time. He is though poor yet honest and hardworking. We all respect him.

# AN IDEAL STUDENT

There are different types of students. But an ideal student is good in all aspects. An ideal student goes to school regularly. He respects his teachers and all the other elders. He reaches school in time.

He wears neat and clean uniform. He cuts his nails short regularly. He doesn't miss any period. He is very attentive in the class. He keeps his books and note books neat and tidy. He always completes his class-work and home-work. He doesn't take leave without prior information and permission. He also takes part in games and extra co-curricular activities. An ideal student possesses all the above qualities.

❏ ❏ ❏

# MY DAILY ROUTINE

I am Palak. I am a student of class Vth. I get up at 6 o'clock in the morning. I then brush my teeth. After that I take bath and wear school uniform. Then I take breakfast.

At 7o'clock I take my school bus. I attend the morning assembly at school. My periods start at 8 o'clock. In the recess, I eat my lunch. By 3 o'clock in afternoon, I come back from school. I wash my hands and face, and then I take some refreshment and watch T.V.

In the evening, I do my home work. Then I play with my friends. At 8 o'clock in the night I take my dinner and go to bed by 9 o'clock.

# MY GRAND FATHER

Shree Shyam Sharma is my grand father. He is seventy years old. He is a retired professor. He is the president of our

'Residents Welfare Association'. He is active and alert even at this age.

He tells me many interesting things. He is fond of reading good books. He is very wise and intelligent. He is very good at General Knowledge. Everyone in the family takes his advice very seriously. Every evening he takes me to the nearby park. He enjoys drinking coffee. All our family members respect and love him very much.

# MY GRAND MOTHER

My grand mother is sixty years old. Her name is Ganga Devi. She is very religious. She wakes up early in the morning and  takes bath. She then goes to the temple. She spends most of her time in reading religious books. She frequently visits 'Satsangs'-the holy meetings.

She is very kind and generous. She loves everybody in the house. She takes care of everyone. She tells me interesting stories at night. She is a nice grand mother.

# MY MOTHER

My mother's name is Mrs. Shalini Khanna. She is thirty six years old. She is smart and beautiful. She has black curly hair.

She is a school teacher. She likes music and good movies. She is a very good cook. She helps me in my studies. She is very polite and kind hearted. She is very pious. She loves me a lot. I also love her and pray for her long and healthy life. She is the best mother and I am proud of her.

# MY FATHER

My father's name is Dr. Anil Sharma. He is forty years old. He is a doctor. He works in Ram Manohar Lohia Hospital. He is kind hearted and generous. He is very hard working.

He is always ready to attend sick people. Sometimes he works for the whole night. He possesses all the qualities of a good doctor. He plays with me. He takes us for outings. He loves me very much. I also love him and pray for his long and healthy life. He is the best father whom I like most.

❏ ❏ ❏

# MY FAMILY

Mine is a small family. It consists of four members. There are my parents, my sister and myself in my family. We have a beautiful house.

My father is a software engineer. My mother is a dietician. My sister is in class V and goes to school with me everyday. We have a small and beautiful car. We go for picnics on week-ends. We all wait eagerly for these outings. We all help each other in our house-work. I am lucky enough to have such a happy family.

# MY SISTER

Dolly is my younger sister. She studies in second standard. She is intelligent and clever. She is the monitor of her class. She is counted among good students. She is  very smart and talkative. She is deeply attached to our mother. She likes to sleep with her. She loves me very much. I also love her a lot.

She likes watching cartoons on television. She is cheerful and calm. She is very systematic and takes care of her things. We all love her very much.

❑ ❑ ❑

# MY BROTHER

Govind is my younger brother. He is three years old.

He stays at home with my mother. He is a very sweet and innocent child. But he is very naughty too. He has many toys but he likes to play with his colourful ball.

He keeps on wandering here and there on his tricycle inside the house. I enjoy playing with him. He does funny things and we all love that. But he has a bad habit of breaking things.

He is the joy of our family. We all love him very much.

# MY HOUSE

I live in a small house in Rohini, North-west Delhi. My house is sun facing. There are three big bedrooms, a kitchen and a  drawing room in it. There are also two bathrooms, two toilets, a store room and a study room in it.

It is open from two sides and quite airy. There are many big windows to let the sun-light and fresh air come in. There is a park at the back of the house. My house is very beautiful and comfortable. We all keep it neat and clean.

M.F. Essays-3

# MY ROOM

We live in a flat. There is a small room in it for me. The walls of my rooms are painted in different colours. My room has one door and two windows. I keep the windows open to let the sunlight and fresh air come in.

My bed is at one corner of the room. On the other side there is my study table and a chair. There is a clock on the wall just above my study table. I keep my room neat and clean. I love my room. I like it a lot.

# MY BEST FRIEND

I have many friends but Vasu is my best friend. He is my class-mate. He is true and sincere. He is very intelligent. He helps me in my studies. He comes from a noble family. His 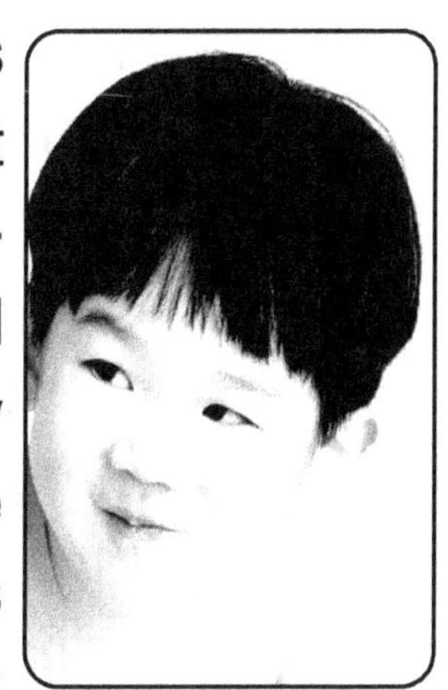 father is a bank manager and his mother is a lecturer.

I am very proud of my friend Vasu because he has good manners and a helpful nature. He is also very proud of our friendship. His company is a blessing to me.

# MY AUNT

I have an aunt. Her name is Shikha. She is my mother's sister. She is the youngest amongst her siblings. She is twenty four years old. She is an air-hostess. She keeps on travelling to many countries. From there she brings different kinds of gifts for us. She is very kind and caring. She visits us on holidays and sometimes on Sundays.

She keeps smiling most of the time. She is very polite. She loves me and respects my parents.

I am also very fond of her.

# MY UNCLE

Dr. Rajesh Kumar is my uncle. He is my father's younger brother. He is thirty five years of age. He is a  doctor. He lives with our family. He works in Safdarjung Hospital. He is very good looking and smart. He is very courteous and hard working.

He is generous towards the poor people. He is fond of thriller movies. He is a sports lover too. I like playing chess with him. He loves me a lot. He brings gifts for me. He has great respect for my parents. My Uncle is no less than a friend to me. He is my ideal. ❑ ❑ ❑

# MY BIRTHDAY PARTY

Yesterday was my 10th birthday. My parents arranged a party for me. We decorated our house. I wore new clothes. I invited my friends and close 

relatives to celebrate the party. I cut the cake. Everyone clapped and sang "Happy Birthday to you".

Refreshments were distributed. Gifts were given to me and I also gave return gifts. We all enjoyed it very much.

# MY NEIGHBOURHOOD PARK

There are many parks in our colony. All of them are well maintained. But the park I like the most is near my house. It has different types of plants in it. It has many flowering plants such as, jasmine, mogra, lily, pansy etc. The flowers give sweet smell whole day.

It also has some trees of mango, jamun, banana and guava. Many birds have made their nests on these trees. It is very refreshing to hear the singing birds. Many people can be seen walking, sitting and exercising in this park. I love this park very much. ❑ ❑ ❑

# THE STREET WHERE I LIVE

The street I live in is long and wide. There are street-lights which keep the street well lighted at night.  The street has a good drainage system.

The street is kept clean. The sweeper comes early in the morning to clean the street everyday. There are two big iron gates at the both ends of the street. I and my friends play many games in the street. People take a walk in the street after their dinner. At night the watchman patrols the street to keep the thieves away. People of different castes and religions live in my street. ❑ ❑ ❑

# THE VILLAGE I BELONG TO

I hail from a small village near Barabanki in Uttar Pradesh. It is about four miles from the railway  station. It is linked to the railway station by a 'Kachcha' road.

Most of the houses of my village are made up of bricks and cement. There are also some 'Kachcha' houses made of mud, stone and straws. My village consists of many ponds, lakes and wells. Most of the villagers are farmers. They live a  very simple and peaceful life. The people of my village are honest and hard working.

❏ ❏ ❏

# MY GOOD NEIGHBOUR

A good neighbour is a blessing. We all are social beings. We need society. Our neighbours play a great part in it. Neighbours can be good or bad.

Mr. Sharma is our next door neighbour. He is a government servant. He has a small family. He is at our back on a call. He is co-operative. He doesn't quarrel with any one. He visits our house regularly. He is always ready to help others. We are lucky to have him as our neighbour.

# MY FAVOURITE BOOK

Books are always considered as the best friend. Books give us knowledge and cheer us up in despair.

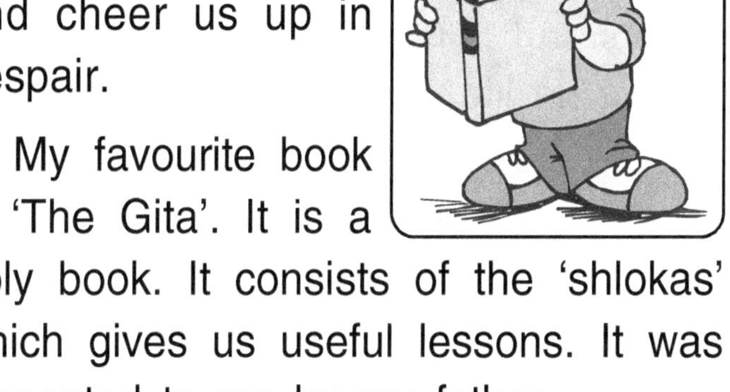

My favourite book is 'The Gita'. It is a holy book. It consists of the 'shlokas' which gives us useful lessons. It was presented to me by my father.

It is a true guide of mankind. Whenever a person is in trouble, it gives him peace and strength. It is a source of knowledge, wisdom and light. It is a gift to the mankind from the God himself.

# MY AIM IN LIFE

Life without a goal is meaningless. One must have some aim in life. Once the aim is decided, it becomes easier to achieve it.

Different people have different aims. My aim in life is to become a doctor. I want to be a doctor because he saves life of injured people and give them new life. It is a noble and satisfying profession. A doctor cures the sick people. I want to help the poor people by becoming a doctor. By doing this I can serve my country as well.

# MY COUNTRY

I live in India. Delhi is the capital of India. It is the largest democracy in the world. It is a huge country. More than 121 crore people live here. India has total 29 states 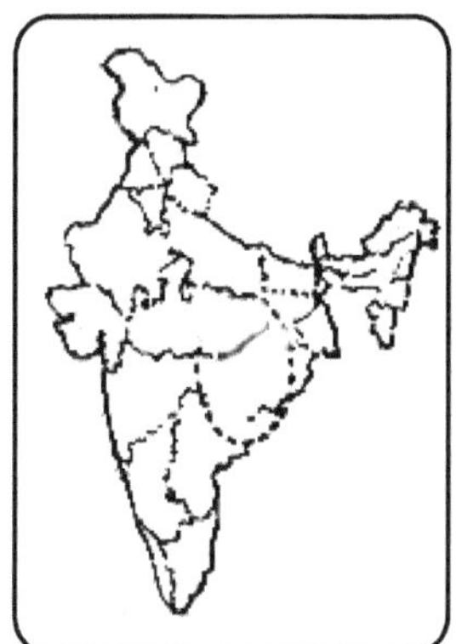 and 7 union territories. There are many rivers in India like Ganga, Yamuna, Kaveri, Godavari, Krishna, Narmada etc. It is a country of geographical diversities. It has many mountains, sea coasts and a desert in it.

People of many faiths and religion live here in harmony. Many languages are spoken here. It possess a rich historical heritage. I am proud to be an Indian.

# OUR NATIONAL FLAG

A national flag is a symbol of pride for its country. India's national flag is called 'Tiranga' or 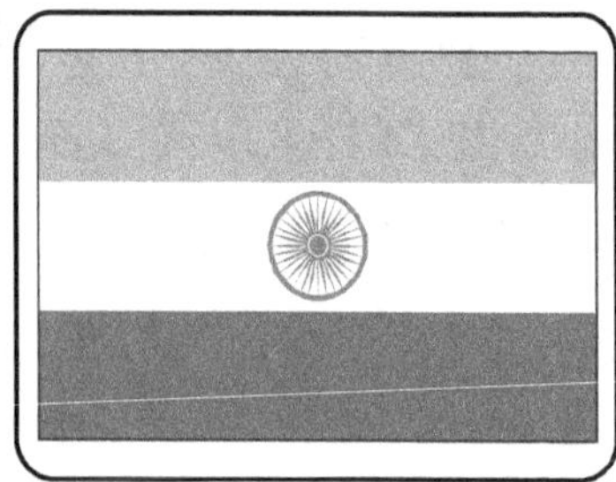 'Tricolour'. It has three equal horizontal strips of different colours.

Saffron is on the top that stands for bravery and sacrifice. In the middle, it is of white colour with a dark blue wheel called 'Ashoka Chakra'. The white colour stands for peace. At the bottom, it is of green colour that stands for agricultural prosperity. It is a great source of inspiration for all of us. Indian flag is hoisted by Prime Minister on 15th August at Red Fort.

# THE INDEPENDENCE DAY

India celebrates its independence day on 15th of August. Our country became independent from the British rule on 15th August, 1947. A  national holiday is observed on this day. Thousands of people gather in the grounds in front of the Red Fort, Delhi.

The Prime Minister of India hoists the national flag here. The people sing the National Anthem. The Prime Minister addresses the whole nation on this day. On this day, schools organize functions and cultural programmes. In North India people fly kites in the evening.

❑ ❑ ❑

# THE REPUBLIC DAY

26th of January is India's Republic Day. On this day in 1950, India was declared a Republic. A national holiday is observed on this day. It is celebrated with great pomp and show.

A huge procession is taken out from the Vijay Chowk near India Gate. The president takes the salute of the armed and para-military forces at the Red Fort. The tableaux of different states participate in it. School children from all over India also take part in it. The procession ends at the Red Fort. In almost every school & institution this day is celebrated with prosperity.  ❏ ❏ ❏

# THE COW

The cow is a pet and very calm animal. It is found almost every where in the world. It is a very useful animal.

It has four legs, two horns, two ears and a long tail. It is found in many colours like white, black, brown etc. It is of different breeds. It eats grass and straws. It gives us milk. Its milk is very good for health. A lot of things like, butter, ghee, cheese, paneer, cream, sweets etc. are made out of milk. It does not harm anybody and is thus loved by everyone.

❑ ❑ ❑

# THE CAMEL

The camel is a big animal. It is also known as 'The Ship of The Desert' because it is an important source of transportation. It has a strong body. It has four long and thin legs. It has a big hump on its back. It has a very long neck, a big mouth and a small tail. It runs very fast on the sand.

The camel eats grass and shrubs. It can drink a lot of water. It can store the water in its hump. It can live without water for many days. It is used for carrying loads and riding. The camel is the only animal that can live in the deserts with ease. ❏ ❏ ❏

# A CAT

I have a pet cat. It is very lovely and docile. Its name is Pussy. She is my very good friend. It has four legs, two ears and a tail. She looks like a little tiger. I feed Pussy with milk and bread. It

follows me everywhere at my home. I like to play with Pussy. It can run very fast. She often sleeps on my bed at night.

She welcomes me when I return from the school. She likes playing with the ball. She also keeps mice away from our home. I like Pussy very much.

# THE DOG

The dog is a  very faithful pet. It is a good friend of ours. It is found almost every where in the world. It has four legs, two ears, a tail and sharp teeth. Its legs are thin. It can run very fast. It can also jump and swim.

The dog eats rice, cooked vegetables, bread and milk. It is very fond of meat and bones also. It has a keen sense to smell and hear. It is a very useful animal. It is always watchful and alert. It watches its master's house. It drives the thieves away by barking and chasing. It is also used by the police in many activities. It is considered the most faithful animal.

# THE HORSE

The horse is a domestic animal. It is found every where in the world. It has a strong body. It has four legs, two ears, a tail and a long neck. It can run very fast and jump well.

It eats grass and fodder. It is kept in a stable. It is a very useful animal. It draws tongas and carts. It also carries loads for us. It is used in riding and playing different games. Besides this, horse is also used in the circus. It is also used by the police force and the army. It serves its master well. The horse is a very faithful and obedient animal.

# AN ELEPHANT

An elephant is a huge and big animal. It has big ears and heavy legs but a short tail. Elephants are of grey colour. It is a thick skinned animal. It has

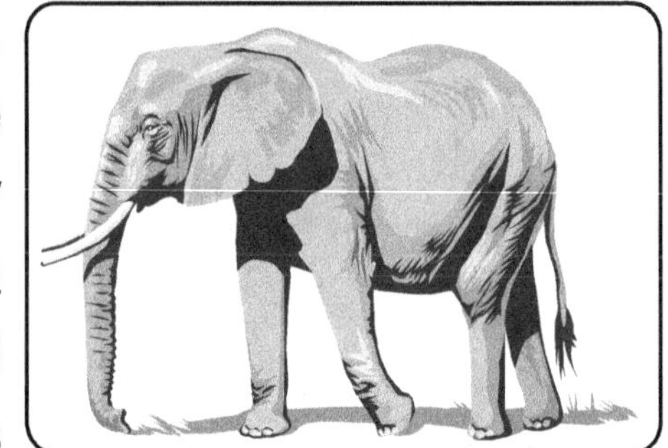

a long nose or trunk with two white tusks. The elephant uses his trunk to grasp things, put food into the mouth and to drink water.

The elephant is a very strong animal. It is very fond of mud and water. Its favourite food is sugarcane. Elephants are trained to do heavy works. It is also used to carry people in the jungle safaris.

# A FARMER

A farmer is the backbone of our country because our country is a land of villages and  most of the people live in villages. The farmer leads a very simple life. He is hard working. He gets up early in the morning.

He works in the field from morning till evening. His wife and children also help him. He works daily and does not have any weekly-holiday.

We all depend upon him for grains, vegetables, fruits and milk. Our country cannot grow without a prosperous farmer.

# A STREET HAWKER

A street hawker can easily be seen every where. He carries his goods in a basket or a cart. He visits every morning and evening. He goes from one place to another to sell his goods. He uses 

different styles to call. When he calls about the things, people come out to buy goods from him. He sells his goods at cheaper rates than the market.

He works very hard for his livelihood. As every hawker is not honest, we should be careful while buying goods from him. Kids wait eagerly for Street Hawkers.

# A NURSE

A nurse is a lady who takes care of a sick person. It is her duty to serve a person who is sick. She is always caring and very active. She is a symbol of services and humanity. She has to do all her work with a smiling face.

A nurse mostly wears spotless white uniform. She helps the doctors. She gives medicines to the patients. She also works in night shifts. She leads a very busy life. We can say that a nurse takes care of the patient like a mother.

# A RICKSHAW-PULLER

A rickshaw-puller can be seen everywhere. He can be seen at bus-stands, railway stations, in markets and on the roads, waiting for the passengers. He can take you to every corner of the city.

He works hard from the morning till late in the night. But still he earns very little. He has to face the cruelty of weather also. Even when he is tired or out of breath, he has to pull the rickshaw. He is not treated well by some people. He is generally hated and spoken to rudely. Some people also underpay him. One should not forget that he is also a human being. ❏ ❏ ❏

# A STREET BEGGAR

A beggar often visits our street. He is lame. He goes from door to door and begs in a sing-song way. He walks slowly with the help of a stick. He carries a big shoulder bag. He puts the collected things in it. People offer him bread, money, clothes and food.

Charity is good but we should be careful. A beggar may be a thief or a robber. He may cheat innocent people. One should know that begging is a crime and a social evil. We must not encourage it. And for this, we should try to take relevant action. ❑ ❑ ❑

# A POLICEMAN

A policeman plays a very important role in our life. He takes care of law and order. He is tall and strong. He wears a 'Khaki' uniform. He  has a leather belt around his waist. He keeps a whistle in his pocket. He has a stick in his hand. Thieves and criminals are afraid of him. If caught, he can arrest and lock them up.

He has many duties to do. He maintains peace and protects our life and property. He is awarded for his work. At night, he is on the patrol.

A traffic policeman regulates traffic. He lives a hard but proud life. ❑ ❑ ❑

# A POSTMAN

A postman is a government servant who delivers the letters, parcels and money orders. He works in a post office. Generally, he wears 'Khaki' uniform. He carries a bundle of letters. He delivers them from door-to-door. Sometimes he brings happy news and sometimes sad news.

His duty is very hard. He has to perform his duties even in odd weather. In the villages, his work becomes more difficult. But he is always very helpful to the villagers. He reads out letters to them. He is very dutiful and works honestly.

# A DOCTOR

A doctor is an important person of our society. He works in the hospital or in the clinic. He cures sick people. A doctor who operates a person is called a surgeon. A doctor is next to God. 

A doctor is always busy and works hard. He helps the people to live a healthy life. He saves many lives. He works for the noble cause. He is respected every where. He is a very important and pleasant person for us.

❏ ❏ ❏

# A SNAKE CHARMER

A snake charmer or 'Sapera' keeps snakes in his basket. He collects money from people by showing them snakes of different kinds.

He looks very untidy. He uses a special flute called 'Been' in his show. He opens his basket and then plays on the 'Been'. He moves it round and round. Then the snake, mostly a Cobra, spreads its hood and starts moving with it. A snake charmer removes the fangs of snakes to make them harmless. It is a cruel thing to do. Now, these types of shows are banned in India. ❏ ❏ ❏

# A CHAIR

I have a beautiful chair. It has four legs and two arms. It is made of iron, foam and wood. It is polished dark blue. My father  bought it for me from Delhi.

I keep it in my study room. I sit on it. It keeps me active and comfortable. I keep it clean. I use it in my studies. I sit on it and watch T.V. also. It is very useful for me. I like it very much.

# A TABLE

I have a table. It is made of wood. It has four legs. It is polished light blue. My father bought this table for me from Modern Market. I keep it in my study room. I also keep my books, note books and school bag on it.

It is very useful to me. I also keep a chair near it. I use it for my studies. There is a table lamp placed on it. It also has two drawers. I keep my pencils, pens, erasers, sharpener and colours in these drawers. I keep my table tidy and clean.

❑ ❑ ❑

# A COMPUTER

A computer is an electronic machine. It has six main parts—CPU (Central Processing Unit), Monitor, Key-board,

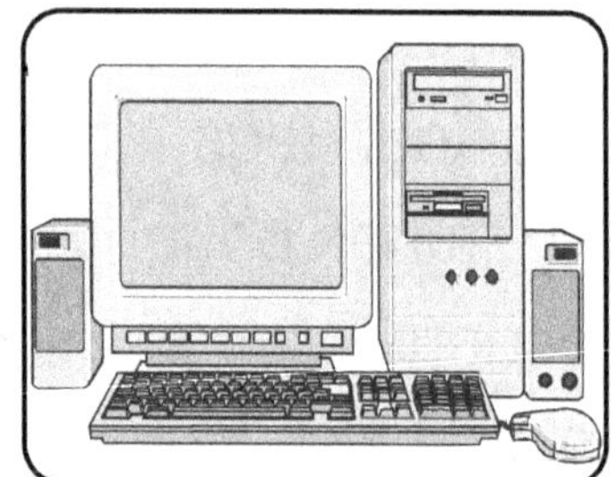

Mouse, Printer and Speakers. CPU is the most important part of a computer. Monitor screen displays the things done on computer. Keyboard is mainly used for typing numbers and letters. Mouse is used to perform multiple tasks like drawing, painting and opening/closing files and folders. Printer is used for printing. Speakers are mainly used for listening to music.

A computer can do many things. It works very fast. It can memorize and store a lot of things. The Computer has revolutionized and changed the world in many ways. ❏ ❏ ❏

# THE RADIO

The radio has its own place even in this modern era. It was invented by Marconi. It is an electronic  device. It catches the signals from a radio station. The station may be at a very long distance.

We can receive many programmes on the radio. We listen to music, songs, news commentary, agriculture and health related prorammes etc. on it. Many educational programmes are aired on it. Nowadays radio sets are very cheap and can be carried any where.

❑ ❑ ❑

# THE FLOWERS

Flowers are very colourful and beautiful. Many of them smell sweet. They are of many kinds. Flowers can be found every where and in every climate. They can be found on land, water,  on the mountains and in the deserts.

Most of the flowers are seasonal. They grow in a particular season. Rose, Jasmine, Lily, Sunflower, Lotus are some examples of flowers. Flowers are very useful. They are used in decoration, gifts, worships, medicines and perfumes. The cooking-oil is also made from some flowers. Honey bees collect honey from the flower. Flowers are the symbol of colour and freshness. ❏ ❏ ❏

# THE FRUITS

The fruits are liked by everyone. They are tasty and healthy. They give us energy and strength. India is very rich in fruits. Almost every kind of fruit is found  here. Mangoes, bananas, apples are commonly grown here. There are many other seasonal fruits like oranges, grapes, pineapples, papaya, watermelon, pear and plum.

The mango is called the 'King of Fruits'. It is very juicy and tasty. Bananas are very common and cheap. Apples are sweet and good for health. Various types of jams, pickles and juices are made from these fruits. We should eat plenty of fruits daily. ❏ ❏ ❏

# THE TELEPHONE

A telephone plays a very important role in our life. It was invented by Alexander Graham Bell. It is a very useful instrument  and has become an important means of communication.

It is a simple device. It has a hand set, receiver and a transmitter in it. It is connected to a telephone exchange through a wire or a cable. When there is a call it starts ringing. It helps us to be in touch with people who are far away. The new version of this instrument is a mobile phone which has many features in it. It is directly connected to the satellite. It is far more convenient than a landline. ❏ ❏ ❏

# THE TELEVISION

A television is one the gems of modern science. On the T.V. we see pictures with sound. It makes  things more interesting and enjoyable. A T.V. has become the must have thing for every household.

We can watch variety of programmes on the T.V. One can surf many channels on it. The range of choice is very wide. A number of movies, songs, sports, cartoon and educational channels are available in it. But too much of T.V. watching is harmful in many ways, especially for the eyes.

❑ ❑ ❑

# A COLD DAY

It was the month of January. The temperature was only two degrees. It was a very cold day. The morning was misty and foggy. People were shivering. Every one  was waiting for the Sun to come out. People were wearing many warm clothes and jackets or shawls.

When fog disappeared, chilly wind had started blowing. It made the condition worse. People were seen sitting around the fire and warming themselves. Some were sipping tea and some were taking coffee. Many people were rubbing their hands to get some warmth. I like winter but the cold should be bearable. ❑ ❑ ❑

# A HOT DAY IN SUMMER

It was the month of May. The Sun was shining bright like the ball of fire. The ground was blazing. The sky was pouring fire. It was a very hot day.

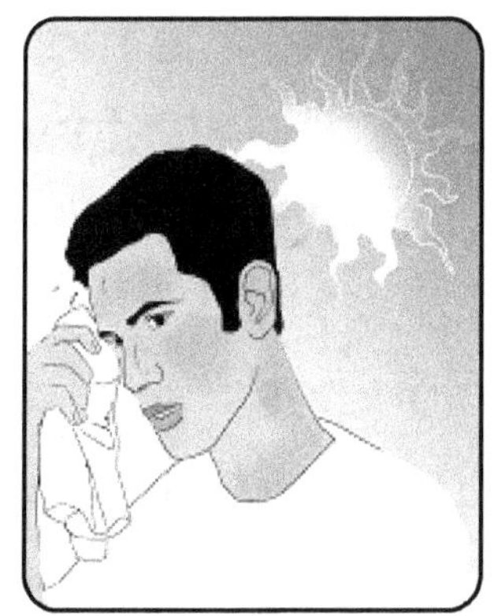

The streets and roads were deserted.

The earth was dried up. Very few people were seen outside. The stray dogs were sitting with their tongues out. Everyone was perspiring and sweating badly. Some people were drinking cold drinks. People preferred to stay inside. I also decided to be at home in front of cooler and enjoyed a cool milk shake.

# A RAINY DAY

It was the month of July. The weather was very hot and humid. The sky was cloudless. But soon the clouds came rolling and it began to rain heavely. It was a  welcome rain for every one. Many people were caught in the rain. They took shelter here and there. Some preferred to walk in the rain.

Children came out of their houses. They were so excited that they started running and dancing in the rain. They played with the paper-boats. As soon as I reached home, I too, went to the terrace to get wet. It was a pleasant day. ❑ ❑ ❑

# A JUGGLER'S SHOW

A juggler or 'Madari' can easily be seen wandering here and there. He earns his livelihood by showing tricks. A juggler may carry many things and animals. He keeps a young boy called 'Jamura' to help him. 

He usually carries a big bag and some baskets. This bag contains many things which are used in tricks. He makes people laugh through his tricks. He speaks in very different and funny styles to attract people. He can make the things disappear in one moment and re-appear them in the other. At the end of the show people give him money.

❑ ❑ ❑

# A MARKET SCENE

I live in Delhi. There are many big markets here. But the Chandni Chowk presents very interesting scene. It is always crowded. People from far and near come here to buy things. One day, I also went there with my father.

First we ate ice-creams and then started buying other things. It is a very historical market. There exist many historical buildings, temples, gurudwaras and mosques. This place is full of activities. We had our dinner at the 'Haldiram' and returned home.

# A SCENE AT A BUS STOP

Last Sunday, at our colony's bus stop, I was waiting for the bus with my  father. Everyone was in a hurry and anxiety. They were impatient to catch the bus. The passengers were waiting in a queue. But they would break the queue as soon as a bus came.

As there was a great rush of commuters, some buses were just stopping only to drop the passengers. There was great pulling, pushing and elbowing at the door. At last we were able to catch a bus. It was a very tiring experience for me.

❑ ❑ ❑

# A SCENE AT A RAILWAY STATION

My uncle was to go to Mumbai last Sunday. I went to New Delhi Railway Station with my father to see him off.

The platform was very crowded. Some people were reading newspapers; some were buying books and eatables. The coolies were moving here and there with the luggage.

In the meantime, the train arrived and people started pushing each other to get into the train. My uncle decided to wait for a while before boarding the train. Soon the guard blew the whistle and waved the green flag. The train started moving. We bade farewell to my uncle and came out of the station. ❑ ❑ ❑

# A SCENE AT A VILLAGE WELL

There is a well in the center of our village. It presents a lively scene, the whole 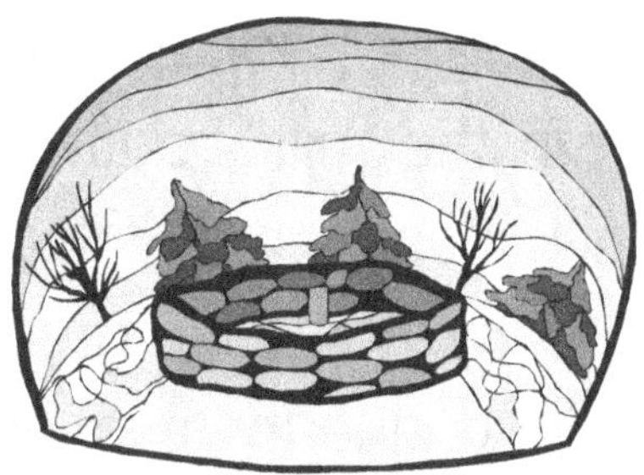day. Long before the dawn, people start coming here. Some come to draw water; some come to wash their clothes and some to bath.

We can see a number of villagers coming here to carry water from the well. They patiently wait for their turn. It is a meeting place too. People come here to discuss various topics. The village well can always be seen crowdy. It is very useful and important for villagers.

# A SCENE AT THE MILK BOOTH

Many people in the city get the milk from the milk booth. There is one such milk booth in my locality. I went there yesterday. It was great rush there. I saw a long queue of people there.

Some people were still coming and standing at the tail of the queue and some were leaving after taking milk. All sorts of people could be seen there. It was interesting to hear their conversation. But it was very boring to stand in a long queue and keep on waiting. At last when my turn came, I took milk and returned to my house.

# A SCENE AT A CHILDREN'S PARK

Last Sunday, I visited the Children's Park near India Gate with my father. It was a beautiful sight. There were many trees all around. At the gate there were a number of stalls. Ice-creams, cold-drinks  and other eatables were sold there.

There were many men, women and children in the park. The children were playing different games on the grass. There were many swings, merry-go-rounds and see-saws. Many hawkers and vendors were also there. I liked the place very much and would like to go there again. ❏ ❏ ❏



M.F. Essays-6

# MORNING WALK

Morning walk is a good exercise. There are various exercises but walking is a suitable and easy exercise for every-body. Morning walk refreshes our mind as air is quite fresh in the  morning. Morning walk can be done by anybody. People wear comfortable dress during walk. It removes laziness. It also gives strength to our body.

It is very pleasing to hear birds chirping and to see the rising sun. After the morning walk we feel energetic. At dawn nature is at its best. ❑ ❑ ❑

# A HOUSE ON FIRE

Yesterday, at midnight, I heard the cries—Fire! Fire! I rushed out at once and went to the spot.  Our neighbour's house was on fire. Flames were leaping up to the sky. Clouds of smoke were rising.

People started throwing water and sand on the flames. In the mean time fire-fighters arrived there. They poured a lot of water on the house from different directions. After an hour or so, they brought the fire under control. There was a great loss of property but no life was lost. The situation was under control after sometime.

❑ ❑ ❑

# A MARRIAGE CEREMONY

My elder sister Palak got married last week. All the friends and relatives were invited at this occasion. A huge tent was raised, which was decorated with  flowers and colourful lights. There were a lot of dancing and singing items.

My sister was wearing a beautiful red wedding sari and golden ornaments. She was looking very beautiful. The Panditji completed the religious rituals. In the morning it was time for 'Bidai' and we all got emotional. After that, my sister left for her father-in-law's house.

# A RAILWAY JOURNEY

During the last winter vacations, I and my brother visited my uncle's place at Mumbai. We took Rajdhani Express from New Delhi railway station. We entered the railway station, boarded the train and took our seats.

The guard blew the whistle and soon the train attained the speed. During my journey I saw many villages, towns, fields, lakes, rivers and bridges. In the train we were served many things to eat and drink. We enjoyed the journey. It took almost 20 hours to reach Mumbai Central station. It was a very pleasant experience for me. ❑ ❑ ❑

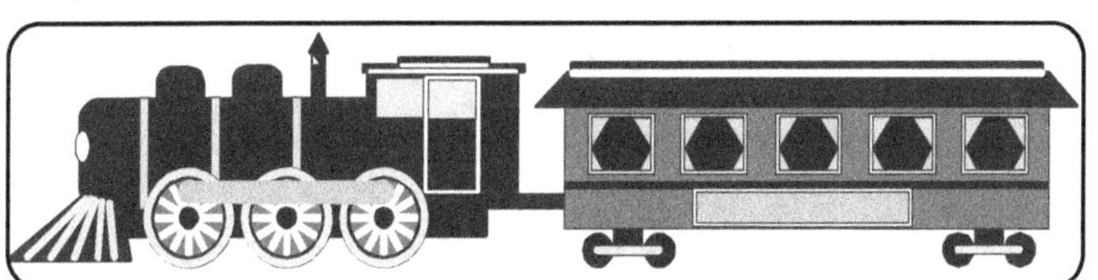

# AN ACCIDENT

It was 2:00 PM. I was standing at the school gate. I saw a rickshaw coming from one direction and a car coming from the opposite direction.

The rickshaw was moving in the middle of the road. The car driver blew the horn and turned the car to the left. Just then, a cyclist appeared and struck against the car and got badly injured. The car driver turned the car to the right and struck the rickshaw. It was broken into pieces. The rickshaw puller was wounded. The police was informed and it brought ambulance with it. All the injured persons were sent to hospital and the car driver was arrested.

# DUSSEHRA

The Hindus celebrate many festivals and Dussehra is one of them. It comes before Diwali in the month of October. It is celebrated for ten days. 'Ramlilas' are staged at night.

On the tenth day, a grand fair is held in a big ground. Shops are set-up here to sell eatables and many other things. In the evening effigies of Ravana, Kumbhkaran, and Meghnad are set on fire. Many people go to watch the event.

This is my favourite festival.

# DIWALI

Diwali is a very important festival of the Hindus. It comes mostly in the month of October-November after Dussehra. On this day Lord Rama returned to Ayodhya after killing Ravana, the king of demons.

On this day, people buy sweets, gifts, new clothes etc. These gifts and sweets are distributed among friends and relatives. At night people worship goddess Lakshmi and god Ganesha. People also decorate their homes with flowers and colourful lights. By bursting crackers, we enjoy the festival.

# HOLI

Holi is also called the festival of colours. It is celebrated in the spring season, mostly in the month of March. People 

enjoy Holi by throwing colours on each other. In Hindu religion this day is considered as the new year's day. They make merry and sweets are served to the guests.

Large group of people can be seen singing and dancing. People embrace each other to wish 'Happy Holi'. Holi of Mathura and Vrindavan is very famous. It is associated with Lord Krishna and Radha. Even enemies become friends on this day.

# CHRISTMAS

Christmas is the most important festival of the Christians. It is celebrated on 25th of December every year. It is also the birthday of Jesus Christ.

On this day Christians visit the churches. The followers of Lord Jesus wear new clothes and attend special prayers in the Church. They decorate their homes and churches. Christmas trees are decorated. Candles are also lighted on this day. Santa Claus gives gifts, toffees, chocolates to the children on this day. Children dance and play with him. Everybody feels very happy on this day. ❑ ❑ ❑

# ID-UL-FITR

Id-Ul-Fitr is an important festival of the Muslims. It comes at the end of Ramzan, a holy month of fasting and praying.

It is celebrated with great zeal. Muslims wear new clothes on this day. They wear a special cap on this day and Pyjama-Kurta. They go to the mosque to offer 'Namaz'. After the Namaz they embrace and greet each other by saying 'Id-Mubarak'. A special sweet dish called 'Sewaian' is prepared. Children are given money and special gifts on this day. It makes them feel very happy.    ❑ ❑ ❑

# GANDHI JAYANTI

Gandhi Jayanti is celebrated on 2nd of October every year. It is the birthday of Gandhi Ji. His full name was Mohandas Karamchand Gandhi. He was born in Porbandar (Gujarat). He is also known as 'Bapu' the father of the nation.

He led us to the freedom. He followed the path of truth and non-violence and the whole world started following his path. Many leaders and people visit Gandhi Samadhi at the Raj Ghat in Delhi on this day. It is also a national holiday.

# GURUPARVA

Guruparva is celebrated by the Sikhs. It is celebrated on the birthdays of their ten gurus. On this day Gurudwaras, the worship places of the Sikhs are decorated. Sikhs wear new clothes and visit the Gurudwaras.  Special prayer meetings are organised. Gurubani is recited with great respect.

People take a holy dip in the ponds of Gurudwaras. Grand processions are also taken out on this day. 'Prasad' is distributed to all those who come to Gurudwaras. Besides this, free lunch is also served.

❑ ❑ ❑

# CHILDREN'S DAY

Children's day is celebrated on 14th of November every year. It is the birthday of Pt. Jawaharlal Nehru, the first prime minister of India. He loved children  very much. Children nicknamed him as 'Chacha Nehru'.

Children wait for this day very eagerly. On this day different types of functions are arranged by the School management. This day gives an emphasis that every child is special. Children play games, sing songs and do many other interesting things. Debates and competitions are organized. Winners get attractive prizes. We all enjoy this day.

# AN IDEAL CITIZEN

A nation is known by its citizens. Good citizens form a good nation. Good citizens can make their country rise. An ideal citizen knows his rights well. But in return he has to perform certain duties.

He can make any sacrifice for his nation. He lives in peace and harmony with others. He always follows the government's rules and regulations. He helps the authorities to maintain law and order of the nation. Thus he is a patriot and loyal to his motherland. An ideal citizen always leads his nation on the path of development.

❏ ❏ ❏

# GOOD MANNERS

We live in a society so we must have good manners. We can win friends by good manners. A person having good manners is always successful.

A well mannered person is polite, obedient, patient and courteous. He respects his elders and takes care of his youngsters. Today if a person is not mannered than he can't achieve the height of success. Good manners make a person a perfect gentleman and he is loved by everyone.

# MAHATMA GANDHI

I like many leaders but Mahatma Gandhi is my favourite. He is also known as 'Bapu' the father of the nation. He was born on 2$^{nd}$ of October, 1869 at Porbandar in Gujarat. His  full name was Mohandas Karamchand Gandhi.

He was truthful from his childhood. He returned to India from Africa and jumped into the freedom struggle here. He led the struggle following the path of non-violence and non-cooperation. He led a very simple life. Gandhiji was shot dead by Nathu Ram on January 30, 1948. He was the architect of India's struggle for freedom. ❏ ❏ ❏



M.F. Essays-7

# A VISIT TO A CIRCUS SHOW

Once, the Asian Circus visited Delhi. The show was held near the Red Fort. I went to see  it with my parents. We reached there by bus. We bought the tickets and entered the huge tent. We took our seats.

The Show began. Some girls showed wonderful feat of gymnastic. They jumped from one side to another. One girl rode a single wheel. A lady walked the rope with a colourful umbrella in her hands. A master displayed his control over the lions. The jokers made people laugh. It was a good show and I can not forget this circus for a very long time.

❏ ❏ ❏

# A VISIT TO AN EXHIBITION

Last Sunday, I went to see an exhibition at Pragati Maidan with my parents and sisters. The whole exhibition was divided into many parts called pavilions. Every state had its own pavilion, selling their traditional as well as new items. They also had their food stalls selling their regional dishes. We visited some of those pavilions.

Many pavilions were also set up by different industries. There was also a defence pavilion attracting a large crowd. We too visited it. We all were feeling very tired. We ate our dinner in a restaurant there and returned home.

# A VISIT TO
# A HISTORICAL BUILDING
# (THE TAJ)

Last Sunday, I went to Agra to see the Taj Mahal. The Taj stands on the bank of the  river Yamuna. It was built by the Mughal Emperor Shahjahan in sweet memory of his wife, Mumtaj Mahal. It is made of pure white marble. The building has a tomb in its center and four tall Minars in the four corners.

The emperor and the empress lay burried side-by-side. Twenty thousand workmen worked day and night to build the historic monument. It was included in the Seven Wonders of the World in 2007. ❏ ❏ ❏

# A VISIT TO A FAIR

Fairs are very common in India. But I hadn't seen any of these, like this Baisakhi. I asked my father to take me to the Baisakhi fair. It was held at Dilli Haat in Pitampura. We hired an auto  rickshaw to reach there. There were many stalls selling different things. People were busy in buying things of their requirement.

There was a lot of rush at the food stalls. We also saw many swings and rides there. I enjoyed some of those which were really exciting and enjoying. After having dinner there, we returned home. ❑ ❑ ❑

# A VISIT TO A HILL STATION

During my last summer vacation, I visited Shimla with my parents.

We were there for a week. It is a beautiful hill station. The climate of Shimla was very good. It was pleasant in the morning but the nights were very cold.

We visited many places there. We saw a big Church at the Ridge Road. I also enjoyed horse riding there. We walked on the Mall Road and visited many shops there. We also visited the highest peak of Shimla the 'Jakhu Hill'. We saw many monkeys in a temple there. It was a refreshing trip for all of us. ❑ ❑ ❑

# A VISIT TO A MUSEUM

Last Sunday, my class was taken to the National Museum on an educational trip. It is situated in New Delhi. It is a huge building divided into different sections.

First of all we saw our galaxy of stars. We felt that we were actually in the galaxy. After that we saw another section. It had weapons of ancient times. There were many swords, bows, arrows, daggers, spikes, helmets etc. The adjacent room had house-hold goods of the ancient era. We saw pots, pans, ornaments and many other items. In the last section, there were many Indian items. After seeing them one can estimate the progress made by the Indians after the independence.

❑ ❑ ❑

# A VISIT TO A ZOO

Last Sunday, I visited a zoo with my parents. First of all we saw cranes,  ducks, drakes, geese and swans in the pond. In the large field deer, giraffes and zebras were roaming. Then we saw chimpanzees and monkeys on the trees.

We were very anxious to see the lions. They were in big iron cages. We also saw jaguars and tigers with their cubs and there was a white tiger too. Then we saw elephants, crocodiles, rhinoceros and hippopotamus. We also went to see birds and there were many of those like parrots, hornbills, owls, pigeons etc. We were very tired when we returned home. ❏ ❏ ❏

# POCKET MONEY

The money, we get from our parents, is called pocket money. It is always welcomed. We can spend it  according to our will. We can buy toys, sweets, books, pens or any other article.

We should learn how to spend it wisely. A penny saved is a penny earned. One should know that it is very difficult to earn money. We should take the guidance of our parents to spend the pocket money. We should try our best to save the maximum of the pocket money we receive.

# HEALTH IS WEALTH

Health is the normal good condition of someone's body. Healthy body is the home of a healthy mind. Good health is a great blessing. If health is lost every thing is lost. Good health paves the way to success. It also provides peace to our mind. A healthy person can achieve his goal very easily.

Healthy people are the backbone of their country. Only healthy citizens can form a healthy nation. A healthy person releases his duty very well. For gaining health we need to take proper diet.

# HEALTHY DIET

It's an old saying 'Nothing is impossible for the man of will and everything is impossible if a man is ill'. To be healthy and fit 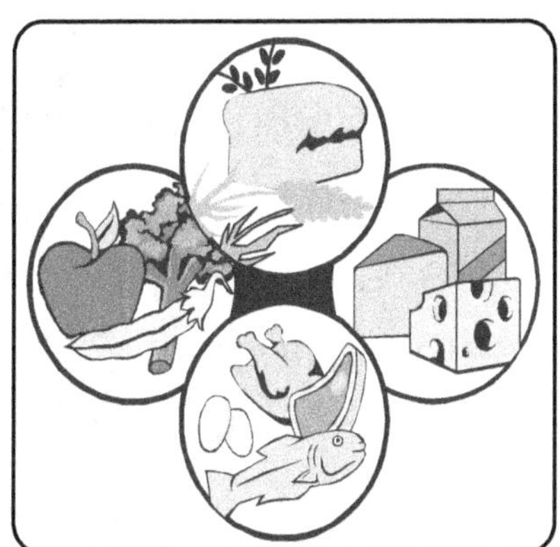 we must regularize our diet. Diet should be balanced and proper. Balanced Diet consists of carbohydrates, proteins and fats in the ratio of 4:1:1 respectively.

We should eat enough of green vegetables, pulses, fruits and salad daily. We should also take milk and milk products. If a person is a non-vegetarian then he should eat fish, chicken and eggs daily. A balanced diet makes us strong and keeps us away from various diseases. ❑ ❑ ❑

# CINEMA

Cinema is a popular means of entertainment. There are many cinema houses everywhere. The  educational values of the cinema is great. It helps us in knowing and solving the social problems. We can know many things about the other countries through the cinema.

The most popular type of cinema is comedy. It is liked by all age groups. A number of movies are made these days. But we should watch only meaningful movies. Cinema is an easy means to reach the public. Today, it is very useful in giving messages and information and is really entertaining. ❑ ❑ ❑

# GARDENING

Gardening is my hobby. There is a piece of land behind our house. I have turned it into a small garden. It is divided into four parts. In its first part, I have grown many flower plants. These give very pleasant smell. In the second part, there are some vegetable plants.

Its third part contains fruits like banana and papaya trees. The fourth and last part is a grassy plot. In the morning it feels very refreshing there. In the evening I water the garden. Gardening gives me a lot of satisfaction.

❏ ❏ ❏

# THE METRO TRAIN

The Metro train has become a symbol of pride for Delhi. It is a big achievement for all of us. The Metro train promises to provide

a solution to Delhi's heavy and complex traffic system. And when the traffic will reduce on roads, it will bring down the pollution level considerably. The Metro train has come as a great boon to those who travel long distances everyday.

The Metro train is eco-friendly too as it runs on electricity. It helps the commuters to reach their destination faster. The Metro train is fast becoming the lifeline for Delhiites. ❑ ❑ ❑

# IF I WERE A DOCTOR

Everybody wants to enjoy respect in society. After all I am not an exception. I wish to be a doctor because I know it well that a doctor is second to the God for an 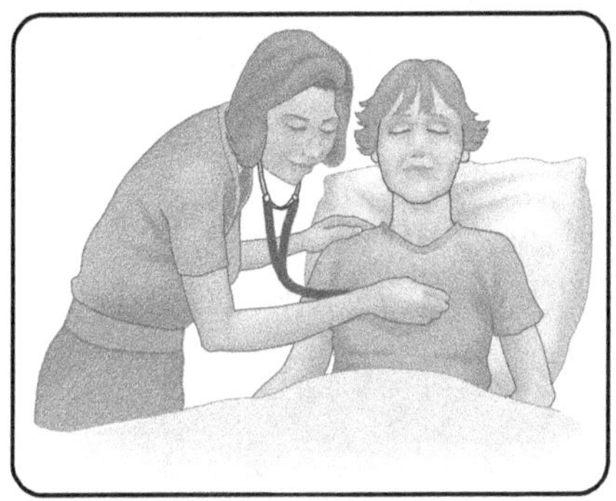 ailing person. If I were a doctor, I would start a small clinic in some village. Most of our villages are without a doctor.

People living in villages suffer from many diseases. Many of them die in want of medical aid. I shall work with missionary spirit. I shall not charge any fee from the poor patients. May God help me to turn my wish into reality!

# IMPORTANCE OF TREES

Trees are one of the most valuable gifts of nature to human beings. They are like the saints who live and die for others. They give us shade, flowers, fruits and add to the beauty of the world. They breathe in carbon  dioxide that pollutes our environment and breathe out oxygen without which we would not be able to survive.

Trees are also used to make many things like paper, furniture, medicines. They also provide shelter to the animals and birds. They keep the weather in control. They bring rain, check floods and preserve soil. Thus, it is our foremost duty to conserve nature and plant more and more trees. ❑ ❑ ❑

# POLLUTION

Increase in the pollution level has become the biggest problem of the world.

It is threatening the existence of the human beings. There are many reasons of pollution like growing number of industries, vehicles, population and construction activities.

Deforestation takes place to meet the demand of land and wooden items. The polluted air can't be purified without the trees. The level of water and noise pollution has also increased considerably. Increase in pollution is giving birth to dangerous diseases. So, it is high time that we should check the pollution before its too late. ❑ ❑ ❑

    M.F. Essays-8

# THE VALUE OF SPORTS

Games are the part and parcel of a man's training and education. Games are necessary for an all-round development of personality. Games  keep us healthy and strong.

They also give us a team spirit. Games make our thinking positive. Participation in games and sports improves the physical fitness as well as wellness of the human being. They teach us not to loose heart when defeated. They train us to face the challenges of life in a better way.

# WONDERS OF SCIENCE

The scientists gifted this world many wonders that changed our lives forever.

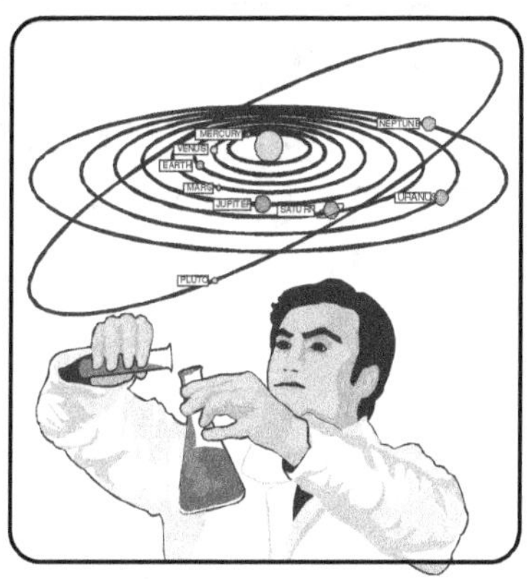


The invention of electricity has removed darkness and made our lives very easy and comfortable. Man has reached the moon now.

The process of printing has been made very easy by the printing press. The television has brought education, entertainment and news direct to our living rooms. The computer has changed our lives in a big way. Because of science many diseases have been conquered. Finally, it is very difficult to count and mention all the wonders of science. ❏ ❏ ❏

# APPLICATIONS

## APPLICATION FOR SUPPLY OF SCHOOL UNIFORM

458/D Sangam Vihar
New Delhi-110062
March 8, 20.....

To
The Principal
M.C.D. Primary School,
Sangam Vihar, New Delhi-110062

Sir/Madam

Most respectfully I beg to state that my father is a security guard. His salary is not enough to support our family. He is not able to buy the school uniform for me. I, therefore request you to grant me uniform out of PTA fund and oblige me.

Thanking you

Yours obediently

Charan Das

# APPLICATION FOR FEE CONCESSION

59B, Dilshad Garden
Delhi-110095
August 9, 20.....

To
The Principal
M.C.D. Primary School,
Dilshad Garden, Delhi-110095

Sir/Madam

I am a student of Vth class of your school. I am a poor student. My father's monthly income is Rs.5000/- only. He is unable to pay my fees. I stood 1st in the class. I am in the good books of my teachers. I shall not be able to continue my studies if a fee concession is not granted to me.

Kindly grant me the fee concession and oblige me.

Thanking you

Yours obediently

Ramesh Kumar

# APPLICATION FOR SCHOOL LEAVING CERTIFICATE

A-5 Prasad Nagar
Delhi-110008
July 25, 20.....

To
The Principal
Salwan Public School,
Pusa Road, New Delhi-110060

Sir/Madam

Most respectfully I beg to state that we have shifted from the above address to 21/A-9 Rohini. My new residence is very far from my present school. I want to take admission in some nearby school.
Kindly issue me the school leaving certificate as early as possible.

Thanking you
Yours obediently

Rajiv Shukla                    ❑❑❑

# APPLICATION FOR THE REMISSION OF FINE

C-1/234 Mahipal Pur
New Delhi-110030
August 4, 20.....

To
The Principal
D.A.V. Public School,
Palam Vihar, New Delhi-110027

Sir/Madam

I am a student of class V-B of your school. My Math teacher was to take remedial class at 2 o'clock in the afternoon. I didn't have a watch so I reached the class late. The teacher fined me Rs. 20/-. I am unable to pay the fine. I shall be careful in future.
Kindly remit my fine and oblige me.

Thanking you
Yours obediently

Krishan Kant                    ❏❏❏

# APPLICATION TO THE LIBRARIAN REQUESTING TO EXEMPT YOUR FINE

To
The Librarian
Joseph Public School,
Paschim Vihar, New Delhi-110063
October 15, 20.....

Sir,

Sub.: Request for Exemption from Paying Fine.

With due respect I beg to state that a fine of Rs. 20/- has been imposed on me for not returning the library books on time. I didn't delay the return knowingly. I was on sick leave for ten days. So I was unable to come to school for returning the books.
I therefore, request you to please remit my fine. I shall be grateful to you for this act of kindness.

Thanking you,

Yours obediently

Rohit Malhotra

# APPLICATION TO THE LIBRARIAN TO ISSUE YOU A DUPLICATE LIBRARY CARD

The Librarian
Thomas Public School,
Mayfair Garden, New Delhi
November 16, 20.....

Sir/Madam,

Sub.: Request for a duplicate library card

With due respect I wish to state that I have lost my library card No. TLN-210/18. It came to my notice yesterday when I reached home and did not find it in my drawer. Perhaps I lost it on my way back home.
You are requested to please issue me a duplicate library card and ensure that no book is issued on my previous card in future.

Thanking you
Yours obediently

Yash                                    ❑❑❑

# APPLICATION TO THE PRINCIPAL FOR EXTRA CLASS

To
The Principal
Sun Shine Public School,
Janak Puri, New Delhi-110058
December 14, 20.....

Sir/Madam

As you know, our Mathematics teacher has not been taking our class since 18th July, 2008. He is suffering from jaundice and has been on leave. The substitute teachers are not serious. Our course is incomplete and annual examinations are approaching.

Kindly arrange some extra classes for us.

Thanking you
Yours obediently

Anand Rathi

# APPLICATION FOR LEAVE

291, Defence Colony
New Delhi- 110024
April 4, 20.....

To

The Principal
Hillwood Public School,
Lajpat Nagar, New Delhi

Sir/Madam

With due respect, I beg to say that the marriage ceremony of my brother will take place on 11$^{th}$ of April, ..... . I shall therefore not be able to attend the school from 8$^{th}$ April, ..... to 12$^{th}$ April, ...... .
Kindly grant me leave for five days and oblige me.

Thanking you
Yours obediently

Kunal Singh                                        ❏ ❏ ❏

# APPLICATION FOR SICK LEAVE

151-B Karol Bagh
New Delhi- 110005
August 6, 20.....

To
The Principal
Khalsa Public School,
Dev Nagar, New Delhi-110026

Sir/Madam

Most respectfully, I beg to say that I have been suffering from fever since August 6, ..... . The doctor has advised me bed rest for three days. So I am not able to come to the school.

Kindly grant me leave for three days from 6th of August to 8th of August.

Thanking you
Yours obediently

Satbir Singh ❏ ❏ ❏

# APPLICATION FOR THE CHANGE OF SECTION

D12, Dayanand Colony,
New Delhi-110024
July 29, 20.....

To
The Principal
Jesus & Mary School,
Safdarjang Enclave, New Delhi

Sir/Madam

With due respect I beg to state that my sister Malini, and I are the students of class V-A and V-B respectively of your school. We have only one set of books. My father is a poor man. He cannot buy us another set of books.
Kindly change either my or my sister's section so that both of us can use the same books.

Thanking you
Yours obediently

Shalini Joseph                              ❑ ❑ ❑

# APPLICATION TO ARRANGE DRINKING WATER

112/BD Jwala Nagar
Delhi-110032
August 12, 20.....

To
The Principal
Baburam School,
Shahadra, Delhi-110032

Sir/Madam

With due respect, I want to bring to your kind notice that drinking water is not available in our school. Whatever water is stored, in the little tank, is finished by the recess. A large number of students remain thirsty.
I, therefore request you to arrange sufficient drinking water for us.

Thanking you
Yours obediently

Sachin Garg ❏ ❏ ❏

# APPLICATION TO YOUR PRINCIPAL REQUESTING HIM TO GRANT YOU LEAVE FOR FIVE DAYS

To
The Principal
Bright Future School
Niti Bagh, New Delhi
September 20, 20.....

Sir/Madam,

Most respectfully I beg to say that my mother is ill. My father has to go to the office. There is nobody in the house to look after her.

I therefore, request you to grant me leave for five days from 21$^{st}$ to 25$^{th}$ of September.

I shall be highly obliged.

Thanking you
Yours obediently

Sikander Shah

## LETTER TO YOUR FRIEND TELLING HIM ABOUT YOUR SCHOOL

B-1/12A Yamuna Vihar
Delhi-110053
23rd September, 20.....

Dear Dinesh,

I am quite well here and hope that you are fine there. As desired by you, I am giving you information about my school. My school is one of the best institutions in the city. The teachers are learned, kind and experienced. They teach us with love and care. Our Principal is a lady of discipline. My school enjoys good reputation in the city.
Please convey my respectful regards to your parents.

Yours sincerely

Ramanuj

❏ ❏ ❏

# LETTER TO FATHER TELLING HIM HOW YOU ARE PREPARING FOR YOUR FINAL EXAMINATION

22, Kaveri Hostel
Kaveri Public School
Ajmer
December 1, 20.....

Dear Father,
I am quite well here and hope that you are hale and hearty there. You know that our final examination is approaching fast. I want to top all the sections. I am working very hard for this. I am taking all the extra classes. I am also going to the library regularly. Still, I need your guidance. Please write to me how I can improve my performance.
Please convey my respect to mother.

With regards
Yours affectionately

Lakshya



M.F. Essays-9

# LETTER TO YOUR FATHER FOR PERMISSION TO JOIN AN EDUCATIONAL TOUR

24, Army School Hostel
Dhaula Kuan, New Delhi
April 25, 20.....

Dear Father,

I am fine here and I wish everyone the same there. My school will be closed for the summer vacation on 15th May, ..... . Our school is planning an educational tour. There will be thirty students in this tour and three teachers will accompany them. Each student has to pay Rs.500/- for this. Also, parents' permission is a must for this tour. Kindly send your permission in writing as early as possible.

Please give my best compliments to my mother and sister.

With regards
Yours affectionately

Sanjay                                    ❑❑❑

# LETTER TO MOTHER ABOUT HOSTEL LIFE

14D, Sangam Hostel
Ganga Public School
Allahabad, U.P.
August 25, 20.....

My dear Mother,

I am fine here and hope the same for you. I have joined the hostel here. The hostel life is quite different from the home. It is a disciplined one. One is to do every thing according to the time table. We are to get up early in the morning and take bath. After this we take our breakfast and set out for school. I come back from school at 2 o'clock, then I eat my lunch. In the evening we play games. At 8 p.m. we eat dinner. After that we sit for studies. At 10 p.m. we go to sleep.
Please pay my best compliments to father and love to Drishti.

With regards
Yours affectionately

Sunny ❑❑❑

# LETTER TO YOUR FATHER FOR REMITTANCE OF MORE MONEY

34C, Green Hostel
Green View School
Dehradoon
August 21, 20.....

Dear Father,

I am quite well here and wish the same for you. We at school are told to buy some extra books and note books. I also need one extra set of school uniform. Kindly send me Rs. 500/- as early as possible.
Pay my best compliments to mother. Love to Priyanka.

With best regards

Yours affectionately

Ishu ❑❑❑

# LETTER TO A FRIEND CONGRATULATING HIM ON HIS SUCCESS

134, Dwarka
New Delhi-110077
June 23, 20.....

My dear Sunil,

I was very happy to know that you stood first in your class. This is the result of your hard work. Every near and dear is proud of you. I am sure that you will keep performing like this in future also.

I congratulate you from the core of my heart on your success.

Please convey my feelings to your parents also.

With best wishes
Yours sincerely

Anurup

# LETTER TO YOUR FRIEND DESCRIBING THE NEW HOBBY YOU HAVE DEVELOPED

16, Akhbar Road
New Delhi-110001
26th July, 20.....

Dear Saloni,

I received your letter yesterday. You have asked me how I am spending my leisure time these days. I would like to tell you that I have recently developed a new hobby i.e. gardening. I have developed the backyard of my house into a garden. We have flowers blooming in all colours and shades in the garden. It gives me pleasure.
Please visit me some day to see how beautiful my garden looks.

Yours sincerely

Tina

❏ ❏ ❏

# LETTER TO UNCLE INFORMING HIM ABOUT YOUR INABILITY TO SPEND HOLIDAYS AT HIS PLACE

24/1A Raja Garden
New Delhi-110028
May 10, 20.....

My dear Uncle,

I thank you for your invitation. But I am sorry to say that I will not be able to come to Ooty to be with you during my summer vacation. Our school is organising special swimming classes during the vacation. You know that I want to participate and win the inter school swimming championship. I hope that you will excuse me this time. I promise you that I will come to your place next year.
Please give my compliments to aunt and love to my cousins.

With due regards
Yours affectionately

Deepali ❑❑❑

# LETTER TO A COUSIN INVITING HIM TO SPEND HOLIDAYS WITH YOU IN DELHI

26/A Anand Vihar
Delhi-10092
May 11, 20.....

My dear Anjali,

I am quite well here and wish you the same. My school is closed for the summer vacations. I am free now and hope that you will also be free soon. I invite you to come to my house at Delhi. We shall enjoy ourselves together. We shall visit 'Adventure Island' and many other places with my parents. I hope you will not disappoint me.

Please give my best compliments to your parents.

With best wishes

Yours sincerely

Sonia                                            ❑❑❑

# LETTER TO FRIEND INVITING HIM TO ATTEND THE MARRIAGE CEREMONY OF YOUR BROTHER

D-16 Greater Kailash
New Delhi-110018
May 28, 20.....

My dear Arjun,

You will be happy to know that the marriage ceremony of my brother will take place on 16$^{th}$ June, ........ The marriage party will proceed to Chandigarh in the morning of 15$^{th}$ June, ......... The "Sehra Bandi" will be held there. I cordially invite you to attend the marriage ceremony. You must reach here by 14$^{th}$ June, ..... .
I hope that you won't disappoint me. Please convey my regards to your parents.

With love
Yours sincerely

Lucky Singh

# LETTER TO UNCLE THANKING HIM FOR A BIRTH DAY PRESENT

B-34 Main Green Park
New Delhi-110048
April 14, 20.....

My dear Uncle,

I hope this letter will find you in the best of your health and spirit. I was happy to know that you remembered my birthday. I celebrated it with pomp and show. All the relatives and friends came to attend the party. I missed you a lot. I received your gift. I was very excited to find a piano in the box that you have sent. I and all my friends liked it. I thank you for your lovely present.
Please pay my best compliments to aunt and my cousins.

With regards
Yours affectionately

Rahul

❏ ❏ ❏

# LETTER TO YOUR FATHER POSTED OUT OF STATION ABOUT HOME NEWS

52-A Tagore Garden
Delhi-110055
August 12, 20.....

Dear Father,

I am quite well here and hope you are hale and hearty there. You have not dropped any letter since you left this place. Every one is worried about your well being. Mother is in good health. Rahul's result has been declared. He stood first in his class. Divya has also fared well in her examination.
When are you coming back? We are missing you badly.

With loving regards

Yours affectionately

Puneet

❏ ❏ ❏

# LETTER OF CONDOLENCE TO YOUR FRIEND ON THE DEATH OF HIS MOTHER

183-A, Ranjit Nagar
New Delhi-110001
February 12, 20.....

My dear Jatin,

I am shocked to know about the sudden death of your mother. The news was like a thunder bolt to me. Last month when I met her, she was in good health. She was like a mother figure to me. I can't forget her love. She was a great lady.

May God grant peace to her departed soul and courage to the bereaved family.

With tears in eyes

Yours sincerely

Suraj Kalra

# LETTER TO YOUR FAVOURITE CRICKET STAR

To

Mr Sachin Tendulkar,
351 A-Esplanade,
Mumbai-5

Dear Mr Tendulkar,

Allow me to introduce myself as your fan. Since the last five years I have been watching live telecasts of Doordarshan of cricket matches in which you play. I am simply charmed by your game.

I have put up posters of yours all over the walls of my hostel room.

My ambition is to meet you in person and be photographed with you!

Yours truly,
Raj Mathur
Class X

Army Public School,
Army Cantt,
Pathankot

# AN E-MAIL MESSAGE FROM A BOY TO A GIRL, REQUESTING HER TO BE HIS VALENTINE

From : sameer@sify.com

To : ishita@sify.com

Subject : Be my Valentine

Dearest Ishita,

I am sure you must be waiting for this message. Would you be my valentine on February 14, (*Year*)? I would be waiting for you at the Beach Club.

It is an earnest request.

Waiting ...

Yours Lovingly,

(Sameer Chaudhary)

# AN E-MAIL MESSAGE FROM A GIRL TO A BOY, ACCEPTING HIS INVITATION ON VALENTINE'S DAY

From : ishita@sify.com

To : sameer@sify.com

Subject : Valentine's Day

Dearest Sameer,

Thanks for your E-mail message dated (*date*). I was overwhelmed to receive it and read your feelings for me.

I would be honoured to be your valentine on this fourteenth day of February. I would be present at Beach Club on that day.

I have so many thoughts to share with you. Please don't miss the date.

Yours most sincerely,

(Ishita Katyal)

❑ ❑ ❑

# AN E-MAIL MESSAGE FROM A GIRL TO A BOY, REJECTING HIS INVITATION ON VALENTINE'S DAY

From : ishita@sify.com

To : sameer@sify.com

Subject : Valentine's Day

Dear Sameer,

I have received your E-mail message dated (*date*).

You are a good friend of mine. I have never looked at you from a very cosy angle. But I have always considered you to be a good and decent classmate of mine.

I would not be able to accept your offer to meet on the Valentine's Day.

We remain friends ...

Yours truly,

(Ishita Katyal)